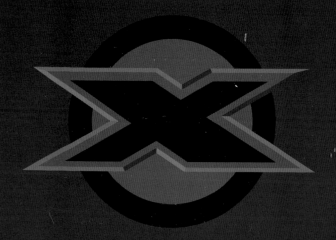

MARVEL
POCKET BOOK

X-MEN
THE HIDDEN YEARS

THE GHOST AND THE DARKNESS

X-MEN: THE HIDDEN YEARS

THE GHOST AND THE DARKNESS

CONTENTS

MARVEL *POCKET BOOK* X-Men: The Hidden Years: The Ghost And The Darkness

X-Men: The Hidden Years: The Ghost And The Darkness. Marvel Pocketbook Vol. 1. Contains material originally published in magazine form as X-Men: The Hidden Years #1-7 & X-Men Vol 1. #94. First printing 2011. Published by Panini Publishing, a division of Panini UK Limited. Mike Riddell, Managing Director. Alan O'Keefe, Managing Editor. Mark Irvine, Production Manager. Marco M. Lupoi, Publishing Director Europe. Ed Hammond, Reprint Editor. Charlotte Reilly, Designer. Office of publication: Brockbourne House, 77 Mount Ephraim, Tunbridge Wells, Kent TN4 8BS. MARVEL, X-Men and all related characters and the distinctive likenesses thereof: TM & © 1999, 2000 & 2011 Marvel Entertainment, LLC and its subsidiaries. Licensed by Marvel Characters B.V. No similarity between any of the names, characters, persons and/or institutions in this edition with those of any living or dead person or institution is intended, and any such similarity which may exist is purely coincidental. This publication is produced under licence from Marvel Characters B.V. through Panini S.p.A. Printed in the U.K. www.marvel.com. All rights reserved. ISBN: 978-1-84653-155-2

X-MEN: THE HIDDEN YEARS

THE GHOST AND THE DARKNESS

JOHN BYRNE • TOM PALMER

Stan Lee Presents

Epilogue:

BEFORE ONSLAUGHT, BEFORE APOCALYPSE, BEFORE PHOENIX AND THE TRAGEDY OF DARK PHOENIX...

BEFORE A MAN CALLED BEAST CAME TO MORE CLOSELY RESEMBLE HIS NAME...

...OR A HIGH-FLYING ANGEL BECAME A RAZOR-WINGED TOOL OF THE ENEMY.

BEFORE A WARY WORLD CAME TO KNOW THE X-MEN AS AN INTERNATIONAL BAND OF EXOTIC ADVENTURERS...

...THERE WERE A HANDFUL OF TROUBLED TEENAGERS AND ONE MAN WITH A DREAM.

WITH MINGLED SHOCK AND HORROR, XAVIER SEES THAT MESMERO WAS IN THE EMPLOY OF THE X-MEN'S MOST POWERFUL ENEMY, MAGNETO...

...WHO NOW CLAIMED TO BE THE FATHER OF LORNA DANE!

THE X-MEN ESCAPE THAT ENCOUNTER, BUT THERE ARE MORE SURPRISES...

...AS SCOTT SUMMERS MAKES THEM AT LAST PRIVY TO A SECRET XAVIER HAS ALLOWED HIM TO KEEP.

THE EXISTENCE OF HIS BROTHER, ALEX.

THE JOY OF THAT FAMILY REUNION IS SHORT-LIVED, HOWEVER...

...AS ALEX SUMMERS IS SOON TAKEN PRISONER BY A MADMAN CALLED THE LIVING PHARAOH.

IN SOME AS-YET-NOT-UNDERSTOOD WAY, ALEX SUMMERS AND THE PHARAOH WERE LINKED...

...AND WHEN THE PHARAOH SEALED OFF ALEX FROM THE SOLAR RAYS WHICH GRANTED BOTH THEIR POWER...

FROM ALEX SUMMERS'S OWN MIND CHARLES XAVIER EXTRACTS THE DETAILS OF HIS ORDEAL.

HE SEES HIM ESCAPE FROM THE MONOLITH, ONLY TO FIND HE HAS LEAPT FROM FRYING PAN TO EVEN MORE DANGEROUS FIRE. LONG BELIEVED BY THE X-MEN TO BE DEFUNCT, THE MUTANT-HUNTING SENTINELS RETURN.

...THE PHARAOH WAS REBORN AS THE LIVING MONOLITH.

...HAD A SON, THE EQUALLY OBSESSED LAWRENCE...

XAVIER IS STUNNED TO LEARN HIS NEMESIS, BOLIVAR TRASK, CREATOR OF THE ORIGINAL SENTINELS...

...WHO HAD CREATED HIS OWN RACE OF ROBOTS TO RID THE WORLD OF THE THREAT OF MUTANTKIND.

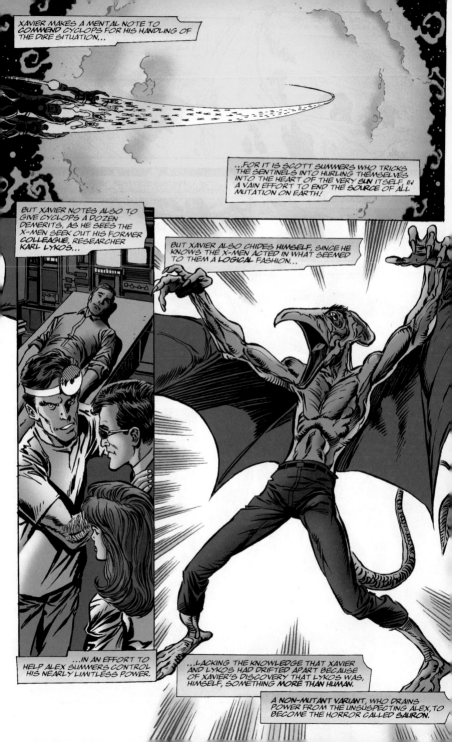

XAVIER MAKES A MENTAL NOTE TO COMMEND CYCLOPS FOR HIS HANDLING OF THE DIRE SITUATION...

...FOR IT IS SCOTT SUMMERS WHO TRICKS THE SENTINELS INTO HURLING THEMSELVES INTO THE HEART OF THE VERY SUN ITSELF, IN A VAIN EFFORT TO END THE SOURCE OF ALL MUTATION ON EARTH!

BUT XAVIER NOTES ALSO TO GIVE CYCLOPS A DOZEN DEMERITS, AS HE SEES THE X-MEN SEEK OUT HIS FORMER COLLEAGUE, RESEARCHER KARL LYKOS...

BUT XAVIER ALSO CHIDES HIMSELF, SINCE HE KNOWS THE X-MEN ACTED IN WHAT SEEMED TO THEM A LOGICAL FASHION...

...IN AN EFFORT TO HELP ALEX SUMMERS CONTROL HIS NEARLY LIMITLESS POWER.

...LACKING THE KNOWLEDGE THAT XAVIER AND LYKOS HAD DRIFTED APART BECAUSE OF XAVIER'S DISCOVERY THAT LYKOS WAS, HIMSELF, SOMETHING MORE THAN HUMAN.

A NON-MUTANT VARIANT, WHO DRAINS POWER FROM THE UNSUSPECTING ALEX, TO BECOME THE HORROR CALLED SAURON.

SADDENED BY THE SIGHT, XAVIER THEN SEES KARL LYKOS HURL HIMSELF INTO AN ANTARCTIC ABYSS...

...IN A LAST, DESPERATE EFFORT TO SAVE THE WOMAN HE LOVES FROM THE EVIL OF SAURON.

FOLLOWING, TO RETRIEVE THE CORPSE OF LYKOS THEY HOPE TO FIND AT THE BOTTOM OF THE CREVASSE...

...THE X-MEN INSTEAD FIND THEMSELVES IN THE PREHISTORIC JUNGLE OF THE *SAVAGE LAND*...

...FACE TO FACE WITH ITS LORD AND MASTER, KA-ZAR.

IT IS HERE THE X-MEN MAKE THE MOST CHILLING DISCOVERY SINCE XAVIER'S SUPPOSED DEATH...

HIS MAGNETIC POWERS FADING, MAGNETO HAS SOUGHT ANY WAY TO REKINDLE THEM...

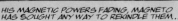

MAGNETO, THE GREATEST OF THE *EVIL MUTANTS*, HAS MADE A LAIR FOR HIMSELF IN THE HEART OF KA-ZAR'S KINGDOM

...BUT HE HAS FAILED, AND XAVIER IS RELIEVED AS THE X-MEN'S MEMORIES SHOW HIM WHAT MUST SURELY BE THE FINAL DEMISE OF THEIR MOST DANGEROUS FOE.

WHAT FOLLOWS SEEMS ALMOST TRIVIAL, IN COMPARISON...

...AS XAVIER WITNESSES THE X-MEN'S ENCOUNTER WITH AN ANGRY YOUNG JAPANESE MUTANT WHO HAS DUBBED HIMSELF SUNFIRE.

THAT ENCOUNTER PEACEFULLY RESOLVED--XAVIER MAKES A NOTE TO HIMSELF TO INVESTIGATE SUNFIRE, AS A POTENTIAL RECRUIT...

...THE X-MEN RETURN TO THEIR WESTCHESTER MANSION FOR YET ANOTHER SURPRISE.

THE DISCOVERY THAT THEIR BELOVED MENTOR DID NOT DIE THOSE LONG MONTHS PAST, IN THE TUNNELS UNDER MANHATTAN.

THAT, INSTEAD, HE HAS BEEN CLOSETED AWAY, DEEP IN THE SUB-BASEMENTS OF THE MANSION...

...PREPARING THE ONLY DEFENSE HE BELIEVES POSSIBLE AGAINST THE INVADING ARMADA OF THE ALIEN Z'NOX.

ONCE MORE the SAVAGE LAND

THUS, NINE HOURS LATER, AS A SLEEK SILVER CRAFT APPROACHES THE FORBIDDING COASTLINE OF **ANTARCTICA**...

"AND YOU CAN DO SO KNOWING YOU WILL EACH RECEIVE TWENTY DEMERITS FOR THIS FAILING!!!"

...THE THOUGHTS OF SOME TURN STILL TO THOSE PUZZLING WORDS...

"TWENTY DEMERITS"?

WHAT THE HECK WAS THAT ALL ABOUT?

DRAKE! YOU IDIOT..!!

LORNA! NO! I DIDN'T MEAN TO..!

NO--YOU NEVER MEAN TO DO ANYTHING, DO YOU, BOBBY?

YOU NEVER MEAN TO HURT PEOPLE--AND YET SOMEHOW YOU DO!

BABY, DON'T...

AND DON'T "BABY" ME, BOBBY!

I'M NOT YOUR GIRLFRIEND! I NEVER SAID I WAS, I NEVER SAID I WOULD BE!

BUT, I THOUGHT... I MEAN... YOU AND I... WE... BEFORE HE...

ENOUGH!

THE PROF!

THE FORCE OF HIS MENTAL ENERGY!

SO... PAINFUL!

SILENCE, LORNA DANE! I AM APPALLED TO WITNESS THIS DISPLAY!

REPORT BACK TO THE MANSION AT ONCE! THE REST OF THE X-MEN ARE IN DANGER, AND WE MAY HAVE TO ACT TO...

DRAKE! WHERE ARE YOU GOING?

WHERE I STARTED TO GO THIS MORNING!

"WARREN IS DIVING, AND HARD!"

STAY CLOSE, CHILDREN!

THERE'S A NARROW *TUBE* OF REDUCED TURBULENCE CUTTING DOWN THROUGH THE CLOUD COVER.

IF WE FOLLOW IT STRAIGHT THROUGH WE SHOULD COME OUT IN...

...IS TO BE *BLUDGEONED* INTO SILENCE BY A SPECTACLE WHICH IS TRULY *BEYOND* THE DESCRIPTIVE POWERS OF *HUMAN* SPEECH.

ELSEWHERE.

DARK SKIES HANG LOW OVER A BLEAK AND TORTURED TERRAIN.

PAIN AND SUFFERING FILL THE AIR AS THINGS MADE ALMOST PALPABLE BY THEIR OVERWHELMING MAGNITUDE.

AND IN THIS PLACE OF SHADOWS AND DESPAIR,...

MASTER! MASTER!

IT IS THEM! IT IS THEM!!

...THERE IS A CENTER OF EVEN GREATER DARKNESS.

MASTER..!

CALM YOURSELF, AMPHIBIUS!

I DID NOT RESTORE YOUR MUTATE POWERS TO HAVE YOU CHATTER LIKE A MINDLESS BEAST.

FORGIVE ME, MASTER! BUT IT IS THEM! THE X-MEN HAVE RETURNED TO THE SAVAGE LAND! WHAT ARE WE TO DO??

DO, AMPHIBIUS?

WE WILL EXACT MY REVENGE, OF COURSE.

FOR WHAT SEEMS THE THOUSANDTH TIME IN THE FEW SHORT HOURS SINCE HE WAS GIVEN THE *TERRIBLE NEWS...*

...SCOTT SUMMERS' MIND RUNS ONCE AGAIN THROUGH THE CASCADE OF MOMENTS LEADING TO TRAGEDY.

IT BEGAN ALMOST A DAY AGO NOW, AS PROFESSOR X ORDERED SCOTT AND HIS TEAMMATES BACK TO THE SAVAGE LAND TO MAKE *CERTAIN* THE EVIL MUTANT CALLED *MAGNETO* HAD TRULY *DIED* THERE, AS THE X-MEN BELIEVED.

IT BEGAN WITH THE SUDDEN LOSS OF STEERING CONTROL IN THEIR SHIP...

SOMETHING WHICH WOULD HAVE SURELY SPELLED THE *END* OF THE THREE *ABOARD* HAD NOT *MARVEL GIRL* USED HER TELEKINETIC POWER TO PROJECT A FIELD OF *MENTAL ENERGY* AROUND THEM.

A FIELD WHICH *CUSHIONED* THEM AGAINST IMPACT, BUT HAD THE *UNEXPECTED* EFFECT OF TRANSFERRING THE FORCE BACK AGAINST JEAN GREY *HERSELF.*

IT WAS THE *CHIEF* OF A TRIBE OF SAVAGE LAND NATIVES WHO DELIVERED THE FINAL, SEARING NEWS.

I AM *SORRY,* MY FRIENDS. WE DID WHAT WE *COULD* TO HELP HER...

...BUT YOUR FEMALE COMPANION HAS *PASSED* INTO THE *LAND OF THE DEAD!*

HE JUST TURNED UP AT MY *DOOR* LAST NIGHT.

NOW HE'S CRASHED ON MY *COUCH!*

YES--I *KNOW* IT'S BEEN WEEKS SINCE THE LAST TIME HE EVEN *CALLED* ME.

HE DIDN'T EVEN SHOW UP TO HELP *VERA* MOVE IN, LIKE HE *PROMISED.*

BUT WHAT WAS I SUPPOSED TO DO? YOU *KNOW* I'VE ALWAYS BEEN A SUCKER FOR THE *BIRDS* WITH *BROKEN WINGS.*

UH-HRRR...

HE'S WAKING UP... I'LL CALL YOU LATER, MOM.

WELL, GOOD MORNING, SLEEPING BEAUTY. FEELING BETTER TODAY?

ZELDA...? THIS IS YOUR APART-MENT! HOW DID I GET HERE?

BEATS ME, BOBBY. BUT YOU *SEEMED* LIKE YOU WERE IN A *BAD PLACE* WHEN YOU CAME KNOCKING AT *TWO O'CLOCK* THIS MORNING!

TWO O'CLOCK?

OH, MAN! I *REMEMBER* NOW! I WAS SO MAD AT THE *PROFESSOR...* I HAD TO GET *OUT* OF THERE!♪

*ANGRY OVER PROFESSOR X'S DECEPTION, WHICH HAD RESULTED IN THEM BELIEVING HIM DEAD FOR MANY MONTHS, BOBBY DRAKE QUIT THE X-MEN LAST ISSUE - JASON

TROUBLE IN PARADISE, HUH, BOBBY?

I THOUGHT EVERYTHING WAS ALWAYS SWEETNESS AND LIGHT AT THAT SUPER-EXCLUSIVE SCHOOL OF YOURS.

YEAH... THAT'S WHAT I USED TO THINK TOO, ZEE.

UH... IS THAT COFFEE I SMELL?

YEAH... I THOUGHT YOU MIGHT NEED A CUP WHEN YOU WOKE UP.

SO... WHAT'S THE SKINNY, BOBBY? YOU VANISH OUT OF MY LIFE WITHOUT SO MUCH AS A WORD...

...AND THEN WHEN THINGS GO BAD, YOU SHOW UP AT MY DOOR?

AM I SUPPOSED TO FEEL FLATTERED OR SOMETHING?

I'M... SORRY, ZEE. I KNOW I SHOULD HAVE CALLED YOU... I SHOULD HAVE LET YOU KNOW WHAT WAS HAPPENING IN MY LIFE...

IT'S JUST... WELL, THINGS GOT REAL COMPLICATED ALL OF A SUDDEN.

I KNOW YOU AND ME HAD SOMETHING GOING, BUT I MET THIS GIRL... LORNA DANE...

AND THEN SHE MET SCOTT'S BROTHER, ALEX...

THIS IS ABOUT ANOTHER GIRL??

YOU DUMP ME WITHOUT SO MUCH AS A WORD, AND WHEN SHE GOES SOUR ON YOU, YOU THINK YOU CAN...

ZEE-- I'M SORRY! IT'S NOT LIKE THAT...

GEEZ, PEOPLE! COULD YOU, LIKE, BE ANY LOUDER OUT...

BOBBY..??

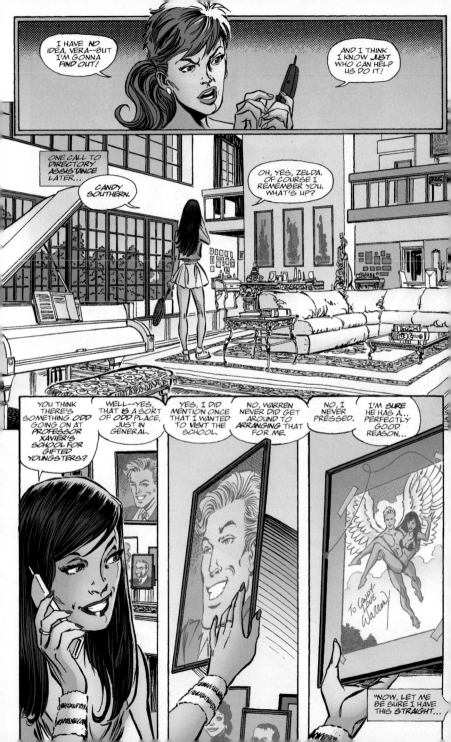

NEXT
On Wings of Angels

"WHILE *CYCLOPS* AND *BEAST* TRIED TO FOLLOW *JEAN* THAT WAY, I TRIED TO FLY *OVER* THE MOUNTAINS.

"IT WAS LIKE TRYING TO FLY THROUGH A HUNDRED *HURRICANES.*

"I WAS TOSSED AGAINST THE ROCKS...

AND THAT'S WHEN THE LIGHTS WENT OUT.

AND YET... THERE WAS... *SOMETHING ELSE.*

JUST A BRIEF IMPRESSION, BEFORE I LOST *CONSCIOUSNESS* ...*SOMEONE... ELSE* THERE?

Y-YOU MUST HAVE BEEN *MISTAKEN,* OUTLANDER.

NO ONE EVER GOES TO THE *HIGH MOUNTAINS.*

TO DO SO IS *CERTAIN DEATH!*

AND YET... AS *BUSTED UP* AS I AM, THERE'S *NO WAY* I COULD HAVE TRAVELED FAR WITHOUT *HELP!*

Y-YOU SHOULD NOT *CONCERN* YOURSELF WITH SUCH THINGS, STRANGER.

SAVE YOUR STRENGTH FOR THE *JOURNEY* WHICH LIES AHEAD.

JOURNEY? WHAT JOURNEY?

"WELL, IF THIS IS INTENDED TO BE SOME SORT OF *TRAP...*

SOMETHING ABOUT THIS PLACE CAUSES INSTANTANEOUS HEALING.

EVEN OF LIFE-THREATENING WOUNDS.

I WONDER WHY KA-ZAR NEVER MENTIONED SUCH A PLACE EXISTS?

AS YOU HAVE NOTED, SCOTT, THE SAVAGE LAND IS HUGE.

IT IS POSSIBLE ITS SELF-PROCLAIMED LORD AND MASTER DOESN'T KNOW ABOUT THIS PLACE!

OR HE'S KEEPING IT A SECRET, KNOWING HOW IT WOULD BE EXPLOITED IF OUTSIDERS GOT WIND OF IT!

YES--DESPITE HIS SAVAGE DEMEANOR...

...THAT JUNIOR LEAGUE TARZAN IS A STAUNCH PROTECTOR OF THE ENVIRONMENT.

AT LEAST WHERE THE SAVAGE LAND IS CONCERNED!

"WE'VE ALL LEARNED THAT THE HARD WAY!!"

YES, ZABU.

KA-ZAR TOO CAN SMELL THE FAMILIAR SCENT OF THE X-MEN ON THAT STRANGE CRAFT.

IN FACT... I THINK I CAN STAND UP...

BE CAREFUL! KEEP THE BLANKET WRAPPED AROUND YOU!

INSIDE? INSIDE WHERE..?

WHOA!

SAKAA! LINAK! YOU WERE NOT TO BRING THE STRANGER UNTIL NIGHTFALL!

WE KNOW, NHU'ABDAR. BUT HIS CONDITION WAS WORSENING MORE QUICKLY THAN WE ANTICIPATED.

DO NOTHING TO REVEAL YOUR TRUE NATURE UNTIL WE ARE INSIDE.

NOT TO REPEAT MYSELF OR ANYTHING...

...BUT WHAT IS THIS PLACE?

A HAVEN, STRANGER. A PLACE OF MOMENTARY PEACE IN A WORLD OF PAIN.

HE KNOWS SOME OF IT, NHU'ABDAR.

PERHAPS IT IS TIME FOR YOU TO TELL HIM THE REST.

IT IS A SAD TALE OF CRUELTY AND BETRAYAL, OUTLANDER.

ONE HUNDRED GENERATIONS AGO, MY ANCESTORS DISCOVERED THIS PLACE.

"AND THEY DISCOVERED ITS WONDROUS SECRET.

"THERE IS A *MAGIC* IN THE VERY *ROCKS* HERE.

"*ENCHANTMENT* THAT *HEALS* ALL ILLS, AND *STAVES OFF* THE ICY HAND OF *DEATH.*

"BUT THERE WAS A *PRICE.* OVER MANY GENERATIONS MY PEOPLE WERE *CHANGED* BY THE MAGIC.

"THEY BECAME AS YOU SEE ME NOW, SLENDER WINGED CREATURES WITHOUT THE STRENGTH OF LIMB NEEDED TO MAINTAIN OUR CIVILIZATION.

"AND SO WAS CONCEIVED A GREAT *DECEPTION.*

"*PASSING BACK* OVER THE MOUNTAINS FROM WHOSE OTHER FACE OUR OWN ANCESTORS HAD COME...

"WE SPUN FOR THEM THE *LIE* OF A *PARADISE* TO BE HAD BEYOND THE MOUNTAINS...

"...FIVE HUNDRED YEARS AGO WE APPEARED TO THE NATIVES AS *PRIESTS* AND *PROPHETS.*

"...ENCOURAGING THEM TO SEND THEIR *OLD* AND *SICK* TO LIVE OUT THEIR LIVES IN *HAPPINESS* THERE.

NOT FAR AWAY...

I'M **SURE** OF IT NOW. MAGNETO REALLY IS **ALIVE**...

...BUT SOME-HOW HE'S **AWAY** FROM THIS PLACE, SHIELDED FROM MY TELEPATHIC PROBES.

IN FACT... THERE'S SOMETHING NOT **RIGHT** PSYCHICALLY ABOUT THIS WHOLE PLACE.

IT'S AS IF THERE'S SOME KIND OF **SCRAMBLING** EFFECT.

I HAVE TO **CONCENTRATE** TO BE ABLE TO READ EVEN THE MOST **SUPERFICIAL** THOUGHTS.

AND BEING ABLE TO READ **MINDS** IS SOMETHING I'VE SORT OF GOTTEN USED TO IN THE LAST FEW...

OH-HH!!

FOOLISH **CHILD!**

YOU ARE QUITE **RIGHT** THAT THERE IS MORE TO ME THAN A **GHOSTLY** PHANTASM!

HAVE YOU **FORGOTTEN** THAT MINE IS RIGHTLY CALLED THE **SECOND** MOST POWERFUL **MUTANT MIND** ON EARTH?

AND THAT THE POWER OF THAT **MIND** IS MORE THAN ENOUGH TO **DESTROY** YOU AND YOUR FELLOW **INTERLOPERS!**

NEXT
Escape to Oblivion

JOHN BYRNE AND TOM PALMER
WRITER – ARTISTS

GREG WRIGHT
COLORIST

JASON LIEBIG
EDITOR

BOB HARRAS
EDITOR IN CHIEF

"AND THERE, SWEPT INTO THE OPEN ONCE MORE...

"...I FOUND THIS STRANGE METROPOLIS..."

...AND ITS EVEN STRANGER INHABITANTS!

"QUICKLY DISCOVERING HOW THE WINGED MASTERS OF THIS CITY TREATED THOSE WHOM THEY CONSIDERED INFERIOR...

OKAY--THAT EXPLAINS WHY YOU WEREN'T CRUSHED TO DEATH AS WE ALL HOPED.

BUT WHAT'S WITH THE GHOST ACT?

"...I UTILIZED A TALENT FOR WHICH I HAD NOT HAD MUCH USE IN RECENT YEARS.

WHICH IS?

SUFFICE TO SAY, IT WILL SEE THE CULMINATION OF THE SINGLE GOAL WHICH HAS DRIVEN ME SINCE THE DAY I DISCOVERED MY MUTANT NATURE!

"I USED THE POWER OF MY MUTANT BRAIN TO SEND FORTH MY ASTRAL SELF...

"...AND IN THAT SPECTRAL FORM CONFRONTED THE LORDS OF THIS PLACE...

"...AND BENT THEM TO MY OWN PURPOSE!"

"...SAVE A SELECT FEW WHO WILL ESCAPE!"

WHAT ARE YOU TALKING ABOUT?

I PAID FOR THIS *CHARTER* TO CARRY ME ALL THE WAY TO *ANTARTICA...*

...NOT LEAVE ME *STUCK* IN *TIERRA DEL FEUGO!*

I KNOW THAT *SENOR DRAKE,* AND IT IS NOT MY INTENTION TO CHEAT YOU.

BUT YOU CAN *SEE* FOR YOURSELF THAT IT WOULD BE *SUICIDE* TO FLY IN THIS *WEATHER.*

THE WHOLE *SOUTH ATLANTIC* IS COVERED BY A MASSIVE *STORM SYSTEM*

THAT STRETCHES FROM *HERE* TO THE EAST COAST OF *AFRICA*

BUT YOU SAID YOURSELF THESE REPORTS MUST BE *WRONG.*

NO SINGLE STORM COULD BE THAT *BIG!*

THAT IS WHAT I THOUGHT, *SENOR...*

...UNTIL THE *EVIDENCE* OF MY OWN *SENSES* SHOWED ME *OTHERWISE!*

BUT I *MUST* GET TO *ANTARCTICA!*

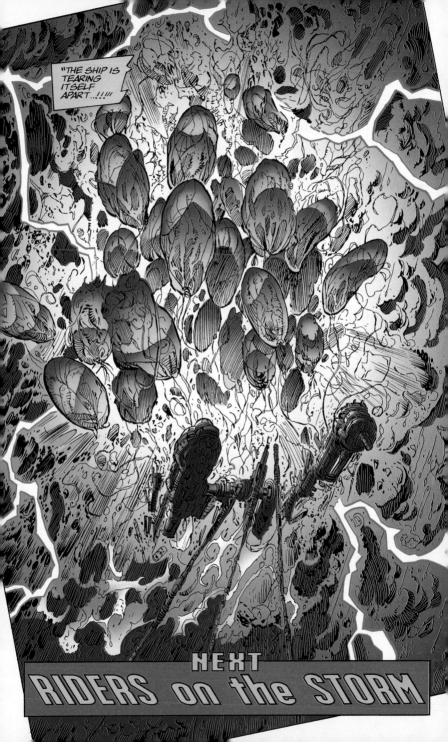

MARVEL COMICS
THE STRANGEST TEENS OF ALL!
APPROVED BY THE COMICS CODE AUTHORITY
X-MEN
THE HIDDEN YEARS
INTO THE
MAELSTROM!

RIDERS on the STORM

THE PLEASANT COUNTRYSIDE BEYOND THE TOWN LIMITS OF SALEM CENTER, NEW YORK.

SO THIS IS PROFESSOR CHARLES XAVIER'S SCHOOL FOR GIFTED YOUNGSTERS. LOOKS A LOT LIKE MY DAD'S PLACE IN DARIEN.

JOHN BYRNE AND TOM PALMER
WRITER - ARTISTS

GREG WRIGHT
COLORIST

JASON LIEBIG
EDITOR

BOB HARRAS
EDITOR IN CHIEF

BUT... WHAT ELSE CAN I DO? THE CHARTER I HIRED TO FLY ME TO ANTARCTICA...

...WON'T TAKE ME ANY FURTHER THAN TERRA DEL FUEGO BECAUSE OF THIS STORM

THE BIGGEST STORM THIS CENTURY--MAYBE EVER...

...STRETCHING ALL THE WAY FROM SOUTH AMERICA TO THE EAST COAST OF AFRICA!

BUT I CAN'T LET IT STOP ME REACHING THE SAVAGE LAND.

I KNOW THERE'S SOME KIND OF TUNNEL THAT CONNECTS THE TIP OF SOUTH AMERICA TO THAT HIDDEN JUNGLE...

...BUT THE LAST TIME THE X-MEN WERE DOWN HERE...*

*IN UNCANNY X-MEN #62 - JASON

...WE FOUND OUR WAY INTO THAT PURELY BY ACCIDENT.

I DON'T HAVE TIME TO SEARCH FOR IT NOW.

WHICH MEANS I HAVE TO MAKE MY OWN WAY ACROSS THESE WATERS...

...SEVEN HUNDRED MILES TO THE CLOSEST PART OF THE ANTARCTIC CONTINENT!

OF WHAT FOLLOWS, LITTLE CAN BE SAID. THE ROARING WINDS SWEEP THE X-MEN FAR--AND FAR APART.

AND AS LONG HOURS CREEP BY AS SEEMING ETERNITIES...

...THE CHANCES THAT ALL WILL SURVIVE TO MEET AGAIN SHRINK IN THE MIND OF HANK McCOY.

UNTIL...

UHHR...

IT WOULD SEEM SHEER EXHAUSTION GOT THE BETTER OF ME!

I LAPSED INTO UNCONSCIOUS OBLIVION LONG ENOUGH TO BE CARRIED OVER LAND!

I'M DROPPING FAST! THE GAS BAG MUST HAVE SPRUNG A LEAK!

I SUPPOSE I SHOULD BE GRATEFUL TO MY GUARDIAN ANGELS THAT MY PRECIPITIOUS DECENT IS NOT OVER WATER.

BUT...WHAT LAND? HAVE I BEEN SWEPT BACK INTO THE SAVAGE LAND, OR...

AT LEAST THE WINDS HAVE DIED DOWN, BUT THAT RAISES ITS OWN QUESTIONS.

HAS THE STORM ABATED, OR AM I MERELY AT ITS MORE QUIET CENTER..?

THOUGH A DISMOUNT OVER MIDNIGHT JUNGLE WOULD NOT BE MY FIRST CHOICE FOR ARRIVING BACK ON TERRA FIRMA!

THIS WILL NECESSITATE A STUDIOUS APPLICATION OF ALL THE SKILLS IN WHICH PROFESSOR X SO DILIGENTLY TRAINED ME!

BEHOLD A GODDESS RISING..!

AT THE END OF OUR PREVIOUS ISSUE WE SAW HANK McCOY, THE MUTANT A.K.A. THE BEAST, LYING UNCONSCIOUS AFTER A STRENUOUS TOUCHDOWN IN AN AFRICAN JUNGLE. *

BUT THIS IS NOT HANK McCOY, AND THIS DESOLATE BEACH IS FAR FROM ANY AFRICAN SHORE.

THIS YOUNG MAN IS BOBBY DRAKE, THE X-MAN KNOWN TO THE WORLD AS ICEMAN...

JOHN BYRNE
AND
TOM PALMER
WRITER -ARTISTS

GREG WRIGHT
COLORIST

JASON LIEBIG
EDITOR

BOB HARRAS
EDITOR IN CHIEF

*AND WE'LL CATCH YOU UP ON THOSE DETAILS AS WE GO ALONG - J.L.

TAKE CARE, GODDESS! IF HE SHOULD ONCE MORE SEIZE YOUR POWER...!

YOU ARE RIGHT, M'KUMBA, BUT IT IS DIFFICULT NOT TO USE WHAT FOR SO MANY YEARS HAS SEEMED SECOND NATURE.

I DIDN'T IMAGINE THAT, DID I? HE CALLED HER "GODDESS", AND...

THERE'S SOMETHING ODD ABOUT THIS. ABOUT THE WAY SHE AND I ARE ABLE TO CHAT SO READILY.

IF I TAKE A MOMENT TO ORDER MY THOUGHTS...

"I THINK THE PLACE WHICH MOST CLEARLY SERVES AS A DEMARCATION OF THE BEGINNING OF THIS SCENARIO...

"...WAS WHEN PROFESSOR X SENT WE X-MEN BACK TO THE SAVAGE LAND TO BE SURE MAGNETO HAD REALLY DIED THERE AT THE CONCLUSION OF OUR LAST ENCOUNTER.

"ONCE THERE, WE DISCOVERED A HIDDEN CITY...

"A PLACE WHOSE RESIDENTS HAD FOUND A KEY TO PRACTICAL IMMORTALITY...

"...BUT ALSO FALLEN IN LEAGUE WITH MAGNETO HIMSELF.

"NOT ONLY WAS HE NOT DECEASED...

"...HE HAD LEARNED THAT RADIOACTIVE LAVA BOILING UP FROM DEEP WITHIN THE EARTH...

"...WAS WHAT HAD STIMULATED THE HIGHER BRAIN FUNCTIONS OF THE PEOPLE OF THAT CITY.

"IN THAT STIMULATION LAY THE SOURCE OF THEIR IMMORTALITY, AS THEIR BODIES BECAME ABLE TO REPAIR ANY DAMAGE OR WEAR AND TEAR."

THE RADIATION ALSO IMPARTED A LIMITED TELEPATHY, MAKING COMMUNICATION POSSIBLE EVEN BETWEEN THOSE WHO SPOKE DIFFERENT LANGUAGES.

SINCE THE BALLOON ON WHICH I RODE HERE WAS FILLED WITH GASES ENERGIZED BY THAT RADIATION...

...IT MUST BE SOME RESIDUAL EFFECT WHICH ALLOWS ME TO UNDERSTAND AND BE UNDERSTOOD HERE...

YOU SEEM LOST IN THOUGHT, STRANGER. ARE YOU WELL?

A WORLD
AWAY...

NEXT

POWER PLAY

THIS ISSUE IS DEDICATED TO ORORO'S OWN "BIG DADDY", DAVE COCKRUM!

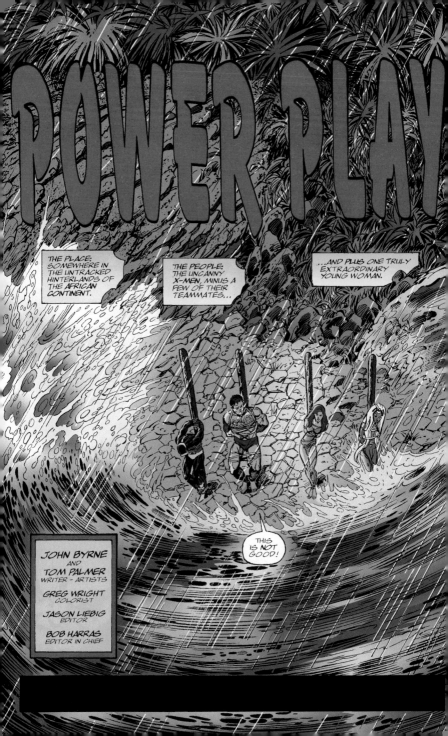

WHAT SHALL I DO?

HE SAW ME IN MY HUMAN FORM ONLY FROM A DISTANCE...

...BUT IF HE SHOULD... RECOGNIZE ME... ATTEMPT TO CAPTURE ME...

UH-HHH...

WHAT... HAPPENED? WHERE... AM I?

AND... WHAT'S WITH ALL THESE... ROPES..?

THOSE ROPES WERE NEEDED IN ORDER THAT I MIGHT PICK YOU UP AND TRANSPORT YOU HERE.

AS TO WHERE "HERE" IS... I AM NOT SURE MYSELF...

...EXCEPT THAT IT SEEMS TO BE THE REMAINS OF A GERMAN EXPLORATORY EXPEDITION.

ONE THAT FAILED A LONG, LONG TIME AGO!

HOLY..!

BUT... UHHN... WHY AM I SO WEAK?

AND... WHY CAN'T I REMEMBER ANYTHING?